DATE DUE

Cats Have Kittens

by Emily J. Dolbear and E. Russell Primm

Animals and Their Young

Content Adviser: Terrence E. Young Jr., M.Ed., M.L.S.
Jefferson Parish (La.) Public Schools, and Janann Jenner, Ph.D.

Reading Adviser: Dr. Linda D. Labbo,
Department of Reading Education, College of Education,
The University of Georgia

COMPASS POINT BOOKS

Minneapolis, Minnesota

Compass Point Books
3722 West 50th Street, #115
Minneapolis, MN 55410

Visit Compass Point Books on the Internet at *www.compasspointbooks.com* or e-mail your request to
custserv@compasspointbooks.com

Photographs ©: International Stock, cover; Cheryl A. Ertelt, 4; Unicorn Stock Photos/Karen Holsinger, 6; Norvia
Behling, 8, 10, 12, 14, 16, 18; Unicorn Stock Photos/Ted Rose, 20.

Editors: E. Russell Primm and Emily J. Dolbear
Photo Researcher: Svetlana Zhurkina
Photo Selector: Linda S. Koutris
Designer: Bradfordesign, Inc.

Library of Congress Cataloging-in-Publication Data

Dolbear, Emily J.
   Cats have kittens / by Emily J. Dolbear and E. Russell Primm III.
      p. cm. — (Animals and their young)
   Includes bibliographical references (p.   ).
   ISBN 0-7565-0059-1 (hardcover : lb. bdg.)
      1. Kittens—Juvenile literature. [1. Cats. 2. Animals—Infancy.] I. Primm, E. Russell, 1958– . II. Title. III. Series.
SF445.7 .D65 2001
636.8'07—dc21   00-011501

Table of Contents

What Are Kittens?

Most people know that baby cats are called "kittens." But most people don't know what mother and father cats are called. A mother cat is called a **queen**. A father cat is called a **tom**.

House cats can be a certain kind, or **breed**, or they can be a mix of breeds. This book is about any breed of cat that lives with people.

◀ Kittens can be playful.

What Happens before Kittens Are Born?

A mother cat carries her babies inside her body for almost nine weeks. She can have up to seven kittens at one time. A group of newborn kittens is called a **litter**. Mother cats have litters in the spring and sometimes in the fall.

The mother cat looks for a nest when it is time to give birth to her litter. She looks for a safe and warm place. A box lined with newspaper or a blanket makes a good nest.

Mother cats need a warm, safe place to have their kittens.

What Happens after Kittens Are Born?

The mother cat licks her kittens dry after they are born. The kittens can't see or hear. Newborn kittens weigh about 3.5 ounces (100 grams). They need their mother to feed, clean, and protect them.

The mother moves her kittens by picking them up in her mouth. The kittens become limp when they are picked up by the back of the neck.

◄ Mother cats lick their kittens to keep them clean.

How Do Kittens Feed?

Kittens cannot see for seven to ten days after birth. But they know how to **nurse**, or drink milk from their mother, within two hours of being born. All the kittens in a litter can nurse at the same time.

Kittens stop drinking mother's milk when they are five or six weeks old. They can now drink water and eat solid food. Also, owners can begin to play with the active kittens.

◀ Kittens drink mother's milk until they are about six weeks old.

What Does a Kitten Look Like?

Kittens look like their parents—only much smaller. A kitten has pointed ears, a wet little nose, and long whiskers. Its front paws have five toes and its back paws have four toes. Some cats have extra toes! Each toe has a sharp claw. A kitten also has a long tail that helps it with balance.

What Colors Are Kittens?

Kittens may have long or short hair. Their fur may be black, red, gray, yellow, orange, white, or a mixture. Tabby cats have darker stripes or patches of fur against lighter fur. Kittens are usually a mix of their parents' colors.

The Siamese cat is a popular short-haired cat. It has pale fur and blue eyes. There are about forty different kinds of cats—cats of many colors.

◀ Kittens from the same litter can look quite different.

What Do Young Cats Do and Eat?

Young cats love to play. They like to romp with other cats, hunt mice and rats, and climb. Cats have a good sense of balance. If a cat falls, it lands on its padded feet.

They use their rough tongues to lap up water or milk. They also use their tongues to keep their fur clean.

Pet cats need plenty of fresh water. They also need food one or two times a day. Young cats prefer to eat smaller meals more often. Many cats enjoy drinking milk and eating fish or liver.

◀ Kittens love to play.

What Happens As a Kitten Grows Older?

Kittens soon grow strong teeth and sharp claws. They can hear, smell, and see very well. They use their whiskers to help them find their way in the dark. These things make cats good hunters and help them to protect themselves.

Cats are also very quick. They can run 30 miles (48 kilometers) an hour when they need to. Remember that cats are related to the cheetah— one of the world's fastest animals!

◀ Whiskers help cats find their way in the dark.

When Is a Kitten Grown Up?

A kitten reaches its full adult size at about one year old. Most adult house cats weigh between 6 and 15 pounds (3 and 7 kilograms). Females are smaller than males. Some breeds of cats weigh up to 28 pounds (13 kilograms).

Healthy and well-cared-for cats can live to be seventeen years old. Some cats live as long as thirty years. Cats make good and loving pets for many people.

◀ A full-grown adult cat

Glossary

breed—a certain kind of cat or other animal

litter—a group of animals born to the same mother at one time

nurse—to drink milk produced by the mother

queen—an adult female cat

tom—an adult male cat

Did You Know?

- Cats are the most popular pets in the United States.

- Canadians own about 4 million pet cats.

- Cats arch their backs and make their fur stand straight up when they are scared. This makes them look larger and scarier.

- Cats are the longest-lived pet animals.

Want to Know More?

At the Library

Evans, Mark. *ASPCA Pet Care Guides for Kids: Kitten*. New York: Dorling Kindersley, 1992.

Fowler, Allan. *It Could Still Be a Cat*. Chicago: Children's Press, 1994.

George, Jean Craighead. *How to Talk to Your Cat*. New York: HarperCollins Juvenile Books, 2000.

On the Web

Cats Magazine

http://www.catsmag.com/

For news about cats and pet care, a chat room, and other resources

NATURE: Extraordinary Cats

http://www.pbs.org/wnet/nature/excats/index.html

For stories of heroic cats, information about breeding, and cat-related games

Through the Mail

The Cat Fanciers' Association, Inc.

P.O. Box 1005

Manasquan, NJ 08736-0805

To order pamphlets about cat health and to find a cat club in your area

On the Road

The American Society for the Prevention of Cruelty to Animals (ASPCA)

424 East 92nd Street

New York, NY 10128

212/876-7700

To get information about adopting a cat from an animal shelter in your area

Index

About the Authors
Emily J. Dolbear has been an editor for Franklin
Watts, Children's Press, and The Ecco Press. She
now works as a freelance writer and editor.
Dolbear lives in Chicago with her husband
and son.

E. Russell Primm has worked as an editor for
more than twenty years. He has been editorial
director for Ferguson Publishing Company and
for Children's Press and Franklin Watts. He now
heads Editorial Directions, a book-producing and
consulting company. He lives in Chicago.